Victorian

Cover: [main] *On the Quay at Leith* by D. O. Hill, c. 1826; [inset] *Robert Louis Stevenson* by Count Girolamo Nerli, 1892.

Endpapers: Loch Katrine, Stirlingshire.

Contents page: Herring boats in Nairn harbour, c. 1890.

First published in 1997 by Wayland Publishers Ltd, 61 Western Road, Hove, East Sussex BN3 1JD, England

© Copyright 1997 Wayland Publishers Ltd

British Library Cataloguing in Publication Data
Foley, Kathryn
    Victorian Scotland. – (Scottish History)
    1. Scotland – History – 19th century – Juvenile literature
    I. Title
    941.1'081

ISBN 0 7502 1962 9

Editor: Carron Brown
Consultant: Donald Gunn, an Education Officer for BBC Education Scotland.
Designer: Joyce Chester

Typeset by Joyce Chester
Printed and bound in Italy by G. Canale C.S.p.A., Turin

Picture Acknowledgements

Billie Love Historical Collection 30; David Livingstone Centre 38; Edinburgh City Libraries 31; Glasgow Transport Museum 26; Robert Hamilton/The Horse Shoe Bar, Glasgow 36 (top); Hulton Getty 36 (bottom); Hunterian Art Gallery, Glasgow 25, 41 (bottom); Archie Miles 33, 40; Nairn Fishertown Museum *contents page*, 24; National Gallery of Scotland *cover* [main] (D. O. Hill); National Trust for Scotland 17, 41 (top); Popperfoto 39 (bottom); Scotland in Focus 15; Scotland Street School, Glasgow 28–29; Scottish Highland Picture Library *endpapers*; Scottish National Portrait Gallery, Edinburgh *cover* [inset] and 21 (top) (Nerli), 24 (George Washington Wilson), 27 (H. J. Dobson), 39 (top) (Catherine Ouless); Richard Stenlake Publishing 11; Topham 9 (both), 18; University of Glasgow Media Services Photographic Unit 19; Wayland Picture Library 8, 12–14, 16, 20, 21 (bottom), 37 (top), /Trinity College, Cambridge 32.

Artwork supplied by: Peter Bull Art 14; Catherine Parsons chapter logo artwork and cover artwork; Mark Peppé 4–5, 10, 22–23, 34–35; Sallie Alane Reason 45.

Scotland

Contents

Victoria's Scotland

When Queen Victoria and Prince Albert first came to Scotland they fell in love with the Highland landscape, which they saw as a romantic picture of lochs and glens. Their love of Scotland prompted them to buy Balmoral Castle in Deeside, in 1852.

After Albert's death in 1861, Victoria published parts of her diaries, telling of their many visits to Scotland. This encouraged more tourists to visit the country and experience its beauty for themselves.

Many landowners built large houses, similar to Balmoral Castle, in the Highlands. The landowners stocked their estates with deer and game birds for rich tourists to hunt. The Royal Family enjoyed hunting, shooting and fishing on their visits and so these pastimes became more popular with the rich. Copying Prince Albert, the rich wore kilts and other tartan clothes.

Queen Victoria visited Balmoral Castle many times throughout her reign.

Soon, the ordinary people found it difficult to move freely in the Highlands. The rich landowners cut the Highlanders off from their estates, gradually taking over their valuable farmland. These changes in the use of Scottish land, known as the Highland Clearances, had a huge impact on many people.

By 1837, the Industrial Revolution was affecting many areas of Scotland, especially the towns and cities.

Before the Industrial Revolution, Scotland had been a farming nation with people living and working in the countryside. Industrialization changed this. Factories sprung up in towns all over Scotland. More factories meant that more people were needed to work in them, so people left their country homes and moved to the towns. The Industrial Revolution took hold quickly and the lives of most Scottish people were changed forever.

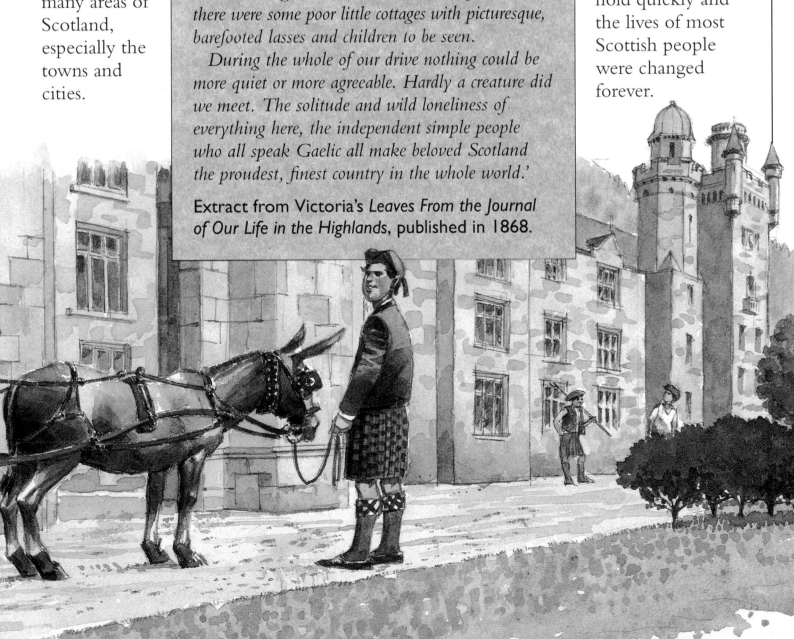

'Ben Lomond, blue and yellow, rose above the lower hills which were pink and purple with heather. We got out and sketched. Only here and there were some poor little cottages with picturesque, barefooted lasses and children to be seen.

During the whole of our drive nothing could be more quiet or more agreeable. Hardly a creature did we meet. The solitude and wild loneliness of everything here, the independent simple people who all speak Gaelic all make beloved Scotland the proudest, finest country in the whole world.'

Extract from Victoria's *Leaves From the Journal of Our Life in the Highlands*, published in 1868.

Industrialization

In the mid-eighteenth century, many Scottish merchants, known as Tobacco Lords, made money from trading in tobacco from America. Ships from America sailed over the Atlantic Ocean and into the Clyde estuary near Glasgow. The Tobacco Lords used their money to arrange the deepening of the River Clyde. This helped the ships sail closer to Glasgow which, as a result, grew as a centre of trade. In 1776, the Tobacco Lords directed their money into the textile industry. With money being invested in industry by wealthy merchants like the Tobacco Lords, and with new inventions, such as steam-power, used in factories and elsewhere, Scotland's factory system grew.

Iron

Scotland's iron manufacture began in 1759 when the Carron Ironworks started production. As the demand for iron grew, foundries were established in Airdrie, Coatbridge and Motherwell.

Iron was used to make the machines in factories, shipbuilding, the steam locomotives on the railways, and everyday items such as cooking pots. Scotland became famous world-wide for its goods made from iron, particularly its ships and railway engines.

This advertisement describes the advantages of the new Carron cooking range, c. 1900.

Shipbuilding

There were shipyards in Aberdeen, Dundee and Leith. In particular, shipbuilding flourished in Glasgow which was close to the areas where coal and iron-ore, needed to build ships, were mined. As Glasgow grew to become the second-largest city in Britain, after London, it was also able to provide enough people to work in the shipyards.

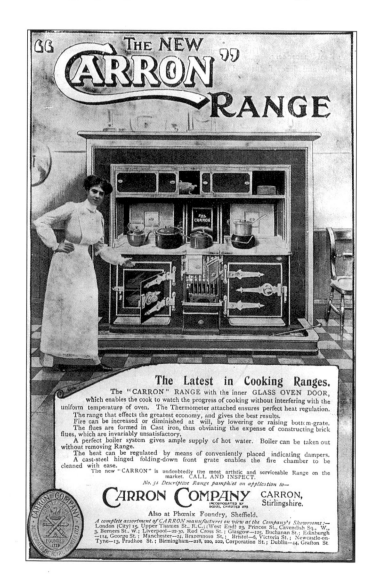

The Latest in Cooking Ranges.

The "CARRON" RANGE with the inner GLASS OVEN DOOR, which enables the cook to watch the progress of cooking without interfering with the uniform temperature of oven. The Thermometer attached ensures perfect heat regulation.

The range that effects the greatest economy, and gives the best results.

Fire can be increased or diminished at will, by lowering or raising bottom-grate.

The flues are formed in Cast iron, thus obviating the expense of constructing brick flues, which are invariably unsatisfactory.

A perfect boiler system gives ample supply of hot water. Boiler can be taken out without removing Range.

The heat can be regulated by means of conveniently placed indicating dampers.

A cast-steel hinged folding-down front grate enables the fire chamber to be cleaned with ease.

The new "CARRON" is undoubtedly the most artistic and serviceable Range on the market. CALL AND INSPECT.

No. 54 Descriptive Range pamphlet on application to—

CARRON COMPANY INCORPORATED BY ROYAL CHARTER 1773 CARRON, Stirlingshire.

Also at Phœnix Foundry, Sheffield.

A complete assortment of CARRON manufactures on view at the Company's Showrooms:—
London (City) 15, Upper Thames St., E.C.; (West End) 23, Princes St., Cavendish Sq., W.; 3, Berners St., W.; Liverpool—22-30, Red Cross St.; Glasgow—125, Buchanan St.; Edinburgh—114, George St.; Manchester—24, Brazennose St.; Bristol—6, Victoria St.; Newcastle-on-Tyne—13, Prudhoe St.; Birmingham—218, 220, 222, Corporation St.; Dublin—44, Grafton St.

James Watt 1736–1819

James Watt, a Scottish engineer, invented the first useful steam-engine, providing factories with a new source of power. His engines enabled the up-and-down movement of a piston to turn a wheel. This meant that factories were no longer dependent on the power of rivers and streams to drive machinery, and could be built away from them. To provide a description of his engines' power, Watt introduced the term 'horsepower' (for example, a '20 horsepower' engine has the same power as 20 horses). James Watt also gave his name to the unit of electrical power, known as the 'watt'.

Dockers were hired by the day or half-day. Although trade was good, there were usually more men available than jobs.

Sailing ships and paddle steamers crowded into the many docks on the River Clyde.

Glasgow shipyard owners demanded high standards from their work-forces. Competition was fierce between the rival shipyards, with each trying to outdo the others by making larger or more powerful ships.

Textile Industry

At the beginning of the nineteenth century, a mill owner called Robert Owen tried to help the workers in his textile mill at New Lanark. He reduced the hours of work, would not employ children under ten years of age, and his mills were cleaner and better ventilated than most. The company houses were well looked after and the streets were often cleaned. A company store was built to sell food and clothes at fair prices. Profits from the store were used to benefit the people of New Lanark. Owen also believed that education was important and a school was built in the town.

However, not many mills were like Owen's. Conditions in most of the textile mills were harsh. Men, women and children usually worked a twelve-hour day. The mills were kept damp so that the threads would not dry out and snap. Workers often had to work in temperatures of over 24 °C. This meant that when the workers left the hot factories and stepped out into the cold, they were more likely to catch illnesses.

Children had to work quickly and carefully on the huge textile machinery.

Children were employed as piecers in a mill. They had to stand watching the spinning machines, trying to spot any broken threads. When a broken thread was spotted, the piecer had to climb between the huge machines to repair it. Accidents were common as clothing, fingers and hair could be easily caught in the moving machinery. Piecers were often punished for their lack of concentration. Sometimes, they were hit with a leather strap, or a bucket of cold water was thrown over them.

Before the Industrial Revolution, all weaving was done at home on handlooms. Then the textile mills, which were quicker, took over. By 1900, handlooms were used only in a few areas of the countryside.

In Scotland, different areas of the country specialized in different cloths. Dundee manufactured jute. Cotton was made in Lanarkshire and Renfrewshire. The mills in Paisley produced shawls based on Indian designs. These designs are known today as the Paisley pattern.

Mining

Mining was an important industry in Scotland due to the many uses of coal. It fuelled the railways, factories and shipping industry and, as the population grew, more coal was needed to heat people's homes.

Coal mining was filthy, dangerous work. Scottish miners lived terrible lives. They were badly paid and rented poor cottages from the mining company. Miners and their families lived in some of the poorest housing in Scotland. The threats of disease and unemployment were always present, and miners also had the dangers of the pit to cope with. Working for a long time in the dusty atmosphere usually caused lung diseases such as pneumoconiosis, commonly known as the 'black spit'.

Children had to push and pull coal loaded into hutches through the mines. The tunnels were often too low for the children to stand upright.

At the beginning of Victoria's reign, men, women and children worked in the mines. A group of inspectors reported on the miners' working conditions. Their report was called the Children's

Air-doors helped to direct air around the pit, helping the miners underground to breathe more easily.

'I go down to open and shut the air-doors at six in the morning with my brother… We get porridge before we gang [go], and take our pieces of bread with us, and come up when the engine stops about six o'clock.

We never change our clothes nor go to school, but we go to kirk [church] sometimes when we have clean clothes. I get 3s [15p] a week, and I give the money to mother… Where I sit is very wet, but I dry myself when home.'
John Duncan, ten years old, trapper.

Extracts from the *Children's Employment Commission Report*, 1842.

'I carry about 1 cwt and a quarter [63.5 kg] on my back; have to stoop much and creep through water, which is frequently up to the calves of my legs. When first down, I fell frequently asleep while waiting for coal from heat and fatigue.'

Isabella Read, twelve years old, coal-bearer.

Steam-engines were used to drain mines and lift coal, but coal was still hewn by hand. Miners continued to work long hours in the dangerous pits.

On 22 October 1877, the whole of Scotland was shocked by a mining accident at Blantyre, in Lanarkshire, that claimed the lives of 207 miners. Few people in Blantyre could have been unaffected by the disaster, losing husbands, brothers, sons and fathers. This was the worst mining accident ever to take place in Scotland. Queen Victoria sent the following telegram:

'The Queen wishes to know the extent of the sad disaster in the colliery, and hopes it may not be as great as reported.'

Sadly, many people continued to die in Scottish mines. About 150 people died each year in coal mines during the nineteenth century.

Before machines were used to lift coal, women carried it to the surface in baskets called creels.

Employment Commission Report. It shocked the government and in 1842 they passed a law preventing all women and children under ten years old from working in the mines.

After this 1842 Mines Act, improvements were made. Pit ponies replaced women coal-bearers for transporting coal underground. New inventions improved the problems of ventilation, drainage and lighting.

Transport

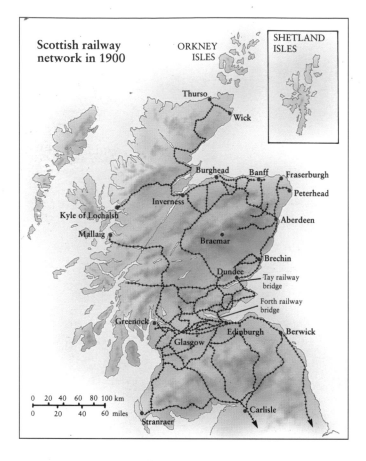

Scottish railway network in 1900

ORKNEY ISLES

SHETLAND ISLES

Thurso
Wick
Burghead
Banff
Fraserburgh
Peterhead
Inverness
Kyle of Lochalsh
Aberdeen
Mallaig
Braemar
Brechin
Dundee
Tay railway bridge
Forth railway bridge
Greenock
Edinburgh
Berwick
Glasgow
Carlisle
Stranraer

0 20 40 60 80 100 km
0   20   40   60 miles

Scotland's transport improved during Victoria's reign. The Forth and Clyde Canal was built in 1784 allowing goods to be shipped across Scotland. Boats could move easily through the new canal. Eventually, horse-pulled barges gave way to faster, steam-powered boats.

In the 1830s, Scotland began its railway network. The railways opened up Scotland, linking its different areas together. The opening of the Berwick and Carlisle Railway provided a permanent link between Scotland and England. The railways were cheap and quick, allowing goods and people to be transported further in Scotland than ever before.

Fort William. Thomas Telford is buried in Westminster Abbey, London.

Thomas Telford 1757–1834

Born in Dumfriesshire, the son of a poor shepherd, Telford became the first president of the Institution of Civil Engineers. He was responsible for planning, designing and building hundreds of bridges, including the bridge over the River Tay in Scotland and the Menai Straits Bridge in Wales. He supervised the building of nearly 2,000 km of road in the Highlands, and the building of the Caledonian Canal, which runs from Inverness to

The Forth Rail Bridge was opened in 1890. It was the first bridge in the world to be built from mild steel, and is protected by paint to prevent it from rusting.

The railways were designed to overcome Scotland's rivers and mountains by building around, through or over them. In 1871, building work began on the first railway bridge over the River Tay. At the time, it was the longest bridge in the world. It has become better known for the dreadful accident which took place in 1879, when the bridge collapsed killing ninety people. The second Tay Railway Bridge and the Forth Rail Bridge were built to higher safety standards, and are still in use today.

Scotland's rail engineering was not only responsible for improving the railway lines, but also for building the engines that powered the trains. Springburn in Glasgow became noted for its locomotive workshops and its engines were sold around the world.

Transport in the cities improved. All the main cities had tram or bus services to allow people to move around quickly and easily. In 1896, Glasgow opened its underground railway to the public. Although London had had its steam-powered underground railway since the 1860s, Glasgow provided the world's first cable-drawn underground railway.

Beautiful Railway Bridge of the Silv'ry Tay!
Alas! I am very sorry to say
That ninety lives have been taken away
On the last Sabbath day of 1879,
Which will be remember'd for a very long time.

'Twas about seven o'clock at night,
And the wind it blew with all its might,
And the rain came pouring down,
And the dark clouds seem'd to frown,
And the Demon of the air seem'd to say —
'I'll blow down the Bridge of Tay.'

Extract from a poem by Dundee poet William McGonegall.

In the City

During Victoria's reign, one of the most dramatic changes to take place in Scotland was the growth of its towns and cities. More Scots were living in the towns than in the countryside by the end of the century.

There were many reasons for people to move to the towns and cities. People were attracted by the prospect of work and a regular income. The cities also offered a greater choice of services, from shops stocking a larger selection of goods to theatres and bars. With a regular income, many people felt that they had more opportunities for a better life. Living in the hustle and bustle of city life made cities places of great excitement.

Sometimes, the move was not such a happy one. Some people were forced to move to the cities. The Highland Clearances drove many people there. Others came after the failure of the potato crops in both Scotland and Ireland. For these people the move to the cities was their last chance of survival.

Life in the city must have been miserable for them. Most of this population had little choice in housing, and were forced to live in the most crowded and unhealthy areas. These areas were a dreadful contrast to the open countryside.

Wealthier people were often unaware of the terrible conditions some people lived in, and were shocked when accounts of them were published.

This tenement building is in Edinburgh. Usually the spaces between the tenements were very narrow and the tall buildings blocked out most of the light.

In 1849, George Bell, in *Day and Night in the Wynds of Edinburgh* described the living conditions of the Old Town area. He writes how the poorest people *'are hidden among the masses of rotten, rat-haunted buildings behind the Grassmarket, Cowgate, West Port and Canongate.'*

These buildings, called tenements, found in all of Scotland's main cities, were several storeys high and provided a cheap and quick way of housing many people. A tenement was a series of 'single ends', one room which was shared by a whole family. Children had tiny beds in cupboards. Each storey was connected by an intricate system of stairways and landings. Families had to share the same close, stairs and back yard. There was a midden for everyone to put their waste, and a few outside toilets.

But there was a positive side. Tenements were small communities, often with families, grandparents, aunts and uncles, living in the same building.

In a tenement, life centred around the kitchen. People cooked, ate, washed and slept there.

In 1858, a writer called 'Shadow' guided readers through the streets of Glasgow. Here he describes some of the poorest parts of the city:

'We grope our way, in an inclined posture, through the entrance to one of those low, narrow closes. A small stream of impure water flows on the right, and with the odour of putrefying animal substances, it smells to suffocation... Of the six or eight families we visit, each occupies but one apartment, in size about 8 feet by 12, [2.43m by 3.65m] containing from four to five inmates, without any regard to age or sex. The bedding, placed in a corner of the room, usually consists of a little straw, and the bed-clothes a few old rags.'

Extract from *Midnight Scenes and Social Photographs*, 1858.

The tenements were built around the shipyards and factories, so people's work-mates might also live there.

For those with money, city life was attractive. They could afford to build themselves bright, comfortable housing in wide, spacious streets. In Edinburgh, examples of this housing can be seen in the New Town. Ornate Victorian flats and town houses were also built in and around the West End. Edinburgh gradually grew bigger, swallowing up the surrounding towns and villages. Areas such as Morningside and Corstorphine became fashionable places for the middle classes to live.

In Glasgow, the middle classes moved out of the city centre westwards towards the newly built Great Western Road, attracted by Glasgow University and the Botanical Gardens. There were large several-storey apartments for the rich, containing between six and ten bedrooms. These buildings were spacious, grand and very different from the inner city tenements.

This photograph shows Jamaica Street in Glasgow, in the late nineteenth century. You can see the types of fashion and transport that were popular. The shops in the street are selling clothes for men.

This poem by Robert Louis Stevenson describes the night-time job of lighting the street lamps. It is an interesting reminder of changing Scotland, as oil lamps in the streets gave way to gas lighting.

The Lamplighter
My tea is nearly ready and the sun has
* left the sky;*
It's time to take the window and see
* Leerie going by;*
For every night at teatime and before
* you take your seat,*
With lantern and with ladder he comes
* posting up the street.*

Glasgow University, founded in 1451, moved to the West End of Glasgow in 1870. The grand, new buildings equalled the wealth and dignity of the university.

Towards the end of Victoria's reign, Glasgow's West End began to suffer from over-crowding, and the middle classes moved further out towards Bearsden and Lenzie. Free rail transport was offered to residents so that they could move to outer areas and still work in Glasgow.

Victorian buildings still dominate areas of Scotland's cities. Impressive museums, galleries, town halls, public libraries and parks remind us of the wealth of Victorian Scotland and its vision of creating a better society.

Health and Sanitation

Industrialization created a new town landscape. Cranes and chimneys dominated the skyline. The factories and foundries poured smoke into the air, creating dirty, smelly, unhealthy conditions in the city, known as industrial pollution.

The crowded cities meant that infectious diseases spread easily. Tuberculosis was common in the working classes because they did not have the good diet and clean air necessary to fight the disease. There was rheumatism too, caused by damp housing and working conditions. Smallpox and cholera were other killers. Cholera spread through water supplies that were contaminated by raw sewage from waste dumped in the streets. The local authorities in the main Scottish towns and cities worked hard to provide clean water supplies. They took advantage of the clean water sources outside their cities. Edinburgh built reservoirs in the Pentland Hills and piped water into street wells and some houses. In Glasgow, water was piped from Loch Katrine about 40 km away.

Given power by the 1867 Public Health Act, the authorities began improving drainage and sewage systems. They built wash-houses and public baths so that people could wash more easily. They also tried to reduce the number of people living in houses, to ease the problems of overcrowding and disease.

This photograph, taken in 1854, shows the resident doctors in the Old Royal Infirmary in Edinburgh. Joseph Lister is the third doctor from the left.

Robert Louis Stevenson 1850–94
Stevenson, one of Scotland's most famous writers, suffered from tuberculosis. To try and beat the disease he and his family moved to Samoa in 1890. He died there. He wrote many stories and poems for adults and children, including *Kidnapped*, *Treasure Island* and *A Child's Garden of Verses*. His work is still enjoyed throughout the world today.

Antiseptic sprays were used to prevent infection during operations. The doctors, however, still wore their everyday clothes.

Scotland's medical training had an excellent reputation in Victorian times, with most of Britain's doctors being trained there. Edinburgh University became famous for its medical discoveries. In 1847, Dr James Simpson developed the use of chloroform in childbirth. In 1860, Joseph Lister used antiseptic sprays to prevent wounds from surgery becoming infected. This increased patients' chances of survival during operations. As these medical advances became more widely used, many lives were saved.

The benefits of vaccination against smallpox had been recognized as early as 1800. In 1864, vaccination against the disease was made compulsory in Britain in an attempt to rid the country of smallpox altogether.

In the Countryside

During Victoria's reign, life in the countryside changed dramatically. It was also quite different for the rich and the poor.

In the Lowlands, farming flourished, providing produce for the busy towns.

By the mid–nineteenth century, land enclosure, drainage and crop rotation had been introduced. The railways allowed tools and agricultural machinery from the factories to be easily distributed across Scotland.

New farm machinery was also invented during Victoria's reign. Reaping machines were produced, with Patrick Bell making one of the first in 1826. Another Scot, Andrew Meikle, invented one of the first threshing machines, used to separate grain from straw. Previously, this was a lengthy task done by hand. However, farm machinery did not create unemployment. Farms could still provide work for people throughout the year due to the increased demand for produce. As a result, Lowland workers were generally well-fed, tall and strong.

During harvest time, travelling threshing machines became a common sight in Lowland Scotland.

Sadly, Highland crofting communities were not as fortunate. Queen Victoria's love of the Highlands dealt a them cruel blow. Landowners began to prefer sheep and deer to crofters. This meant they needed the land the crofters farmed.

So the crofters were forced out of their homes which were then burnt and pulled down. This was known as the Highland Clearances. Some people resettled on the coast or moved to the towns to work. Many left Scotland forever, emigrating to countries such as Canada and Australia. The Highlanders felt much resentment towards Queen Victoria due to all the changes she brought about.

Crofts like this one were homes to farming people. Many were destroyed during the Highland Clearances.

An old fisherman from Nairn, baiting his lines to fish for cod and haddock. By the 1880s, nets were being used to catch herring.

On the coast, people tried to make a living from fishing or from collecting seaweed. Some coastal towns were involved in whaling. Whale oil was used to soften jute and whalebone was used in ladies' corsets and petticoat frames.

In order to make a living, many Highland people, mostly women, travelled to the Lowlands for seasonal work such as hay harvesting, fruit picking or 'tattie howking' (pulling potatoes).

The Crofters Land Act of 1886 protected crofters from further eviction. However, it did not return the land to the people, preventing the Highlanders from returning to the crofting life that had supported them for so long.

'An old fish wife with her creel on her back, her bare legs and feet and very short petticoat began waving a handkerchief and almost dancing as we drove away.'

Extract from *Leaves from the Journal of Our Life in the Highlands*, 1868.

Queen Victoria's description (above) and MacTaggart's painting (below) give a romantic picture of a fishing life. The reality was very different. Life for fisher people was seasonal, unstable and very unsettling.

Making Life Better

Many attempts were made to improve life for people in Scotland. The growing population of the towns and cities meant that there was more crime. So, in the 1830s, a professional, full-time police force was introduced. Large prisons were also built to hold convicted criminals. Many of these prisons, such as Barlinnie in Glasgow and Peterhead near Aberdeen, are still used today.

Fire was a constant threat in the densely built cities, often destroying whole buildings and killing many people. In 1824, Edinburgh established the first city fire brigade, with other cities and towns following its example. Early fire engine water pumps were powered by hand until the 1870s, when steam-driven engines were used.

Safety at work was also of concern to many people. Workers keen to improve

A hand-operated fire engine, like this one, carried its own tank of water.

Keir Hardie 1856–1915

Born in Holytown, Lanarkshire, James Keir Hardie first started working in the coal mines when he was ten years old. He educated himself at night school and then spent his whole life campaigning to improve working conditions for miners and other industrial workers. Hardie used the changing political system to help the working classes and became a Member of Parliament in 1892.

working conditions turned to trade unions for support. During the 1870s and 1880s, trade unions grew in Scotland. Workers, benefiting from new voting rights, took a greater interest in politics and its effect on their lives. Working-class men tried to form their own political party that would represent their interests in Parliament. This was achieved by Keir Hardie who, in 1888, became the chairman of the Scottish Labour Party. This was the first independent Labour Party in Britain.

Queen Victoria wrote letters to the government showing concern for the welfare of the poor. She pointed out that more should be done to protect this part of the population. The Poor Law of 1845 provided help for people who were too young, old or ill to work. Parish Boards collected money to distribute to those in need. Following on from this law many poorhouses were built. These were often unpleasant and strictly run, prompting Queen Victoria to write in 1883:

'The Queen has been much distressed by all she has heard and read lately of the deplorable condition of the Homes of the Poor in our great towns.'

Other organizations also tried to improve people's lives, and many charities and societies were formed. The Co-operative Society, based on Robert Owen's example in New Lanark (see page 10), provided a range of cheaper goods for the working classes. Owen rewarded customer loyalty with cash payouts.

Education

At the start of the nineteenth century, children did not have to go to school. Most girls could not go to school at all until around 1870. They were expected to learn what they needed to know from their parents, guardians or tutors at home.

Only wealthy people could afford to employ tutors or to send their sons to fee-paying, privately run schools. From these schools, pupils were allowed to attend university.

Educating the poor was difficult. Every parish had to have a school, but the growing population meant that class sizes increased dramatically. Classes of over eighty pupils were not unheard of and the quality of teaching varied greatly.

Many people, especially those involved with the Church, were appalled by the lack of education being provided in the cities. In 1841, Sheriff Watson set up a 'Ragged School' for the poor in Aberdeen. Although it could not match the private schools, it tried to provide a basic education for the poorest children. Other Ragged Schools were soon set up.

Each child had to pay a penny a week to go a school like this one.

In 1867, the government realized the need for good education and sent a group of commissioners to report on Scotland's schools. The result was the 1872 Scottish Education Act, which stated that all children between the ages of five and thirteen years should attend school. Local School Boards organized the running of the schools. New schools were built and teachers were given formal training. In Glasgow, David Stow established the first teacher-training college in Britain.

Young children learned to write on slate. Older pupils wrote with ink on paper.

The first Board Schools concentrated on the three Rs: reading, 'riting and 'rithmetic. These were taught by repetition of facts until they were remembered. Later, the subjects taught included French, German, Latin, Greek, geography and science. These subjects meant that more people could enter university and college. In 1892, women were allowed to attend university in Scotland and take degrees.

In 1883, the school leaving age was raised to fourteen years old and most Scottish children received a good basic education. By 1900, most people realized the importance of education. Yet some poorer families could not afford to have their children at school and forced them to leave. They needed their children to work so that the family could have more money to live on.

Work

You have already seen that for many Scots work was hard. People worked long hours, were often poorly paid and had to endure usually dangerous and unhealthy conditions. The government realized that industrial workers were important to the country and had helped to create Britain's economic growth during the nineteenth century. The government passed many laws throughout Victoria's reign to improve working conditions.

Many Scots worked within industries but it is important to look at some of the other jobs people did in Victorian Scotland. The cities then required people to work in the many public services.

There would have been shoe makers and bank clerks, tram drivers and chemists, each helping to run the cities. For women, there were new opportunities as offices, equipped with new telephones and typewriters, required more workers. The need for shop assistants grew as more shops opened up. Each city had a fine collection of attractive department stores, including Jenners in Edinburgh.

In the university towns, there was also a need for people to work in the printing and publishing companies that provided books. These skilled jobs required good eyes and steady hands. Each page of a book consisted of tiny metal letters that had to be set into words and printed.

Shoes were made by hand in small workshops.

This picture shows one of Edinburgh's most famous department stores. Jenners prides itself in providing high-quality goods for its customers, just as it did more than a hundred years ago.

IMPORTANT DATES

1833 Factory Act – limited the hours children allowed to work

1842 Mines Act – women and children under ten years old no longer worked underground

1845 Scottish Poor Law – Parish help for people unable to work

1872 Scottish Education Act – compulsory education for children of five to thirteen years old

After the publicity given to Florence Nightingale, a famous British nurse who worked with injured soldiers in the Crimean War (1853–56), nursing became became an attractive choice of work for many women. Teaching work was also popular. After the 1872 Scottish Education Act, more teachers were needed to work in schools due to bigger classes. Both men and women could teach, although women had to stop working after they married.

At Home

Almost all housework in Victorian times was done by women. It would have taken much longer than it does today. There was no running water, and only a few houses had gas or electricity. Housework was hard, tiring work that took a lot of time and effort as there were few machines to help.

For the working classes, housework had to be combined with a day's work outside the home. Wealthy households could afford to pay servants to do their chores. Servants were cheap to employ. This could be one of the reasons why few devices to help with the housework were invented in the earlier part of the

Although people in service were not well paid, working conditions were better than in mills or factories.

nineteenth century. A typical household employed about seven servants, each with their own duties.

Housework routines were similar in rich and poor households. The day started early with the coal fires being made up and lit. This was a dirty job since the ashes had to be swept and the grate cleaned. Coal fires created a lot of smoke outside the home and dust inside it, which was one of the reasons why housework took so long. The fire in the kitchen range, though, used for heating water and cooking, would not be allowed to go out since it took so long to heat up.

Washing clothes in Victorian times was quite different from today. There were no washing machines or tumble driers, and no soap powders. Very dirty

Everyone helped out on washday. Wet clothes, covered with soap, were rubbed against a washboard. They were then put in a tub and stirred with a wooden dolly. A mangle was used to squeeze out the water then the clothes were hung out to dry.

washing was left to soak in water, often for several days.

Wealthy people could afford to send their washing to a laundry or may even have employed servants to work in their own household laundry. In contrast, washing in the poor tenements was done in the wash-house in the back yard. Because it was such a long, drawn-out task, people who could afford it took their washing to a washer woman who lived nearby.

In Victorian Scotland, something as simple as having a bath was a lengthy task. Water had to be heated on a range then poured into a tin bath. For poorer families, this meant everyone shared the same bath water, with the father usually going first. The bath was placed in the centre of the room, sometimes with a screen around it to save embarrassment. Wealthy people had the luxury of servants, privacy and clean water.

People in tenements had to share outside toilets. Chamber pots were also used, particularly at night. The invention of the flushing toilet in the 1890s must have been a welcome relief.

Keeping food fresh was a big problem. There were no frozen foods, and only a few items came in packets or tins. Wealthier people may have had iceboxes to keep their food cool. As more foods were being imported in refrigerated ships, poorer people could afford to buy new types of food. Wheat from Canada and hams from Denmark were added to their traditional diet of porridge, potatoes, broth and fish. When *Mrs Beeton's Book of Household Management* was published in 1861, it became the most useful book for Victorian women to own. Its recipes told how to use the new foods that had become available.

Sir Thomas Lipton 1850–1931

Thomas Lipton was born in Glasgow. In 1871, he opened a grocery shop in Stobcross Street, Glasgow. His ham, butter and eggs formed a major part of the working-class diet in the city. His success, based on selling *'sound food at a reasonable price'*, allowed him to open more shops in Scotland and the rest of Britain. Lipton used many different advertising gimmicks to promote his business. These included processions taking giant cheeses to his shops and displaying sculptures made from butter in his shop windows.

In 1895, Lipton began supplying tea to Queen Victoria. Lipton's empire had links around the world and it made him very wealthy. His friendship with the future king, Edward VII, made him a regular visitor to Balmoral. Lipton, however, never forgot his poor upbringing in Glasgow. When he died he left almost £1 million to help the poor in the city.

Lipton's processions attracted much interest as they made their way through the city, ensuring that everyone would hear of his grocery shops.

Leisure Time

People in Victorian Scotland worked long hours, but most people did not work on Sundays. A lucky few also had Saturday afternoons off work.

In the early nineteenth century, people were drinking more, so more pubs were built. These were used mainly by men. Most women relaxed at home with their knitting or sewing. Victorian bars were beautifully decorated with stained glass, shiny brass fittings and elaborate wooden carvings.

Bars like The Horse Shoe in Glasgow provided welcome meeting places for their customers.

Sport became very popular in Victorian Scotland. A form of golf had been played here for hundreds of years. However, it was not until the Royal and Ancient Club of St Andrews created national rules and held the first Open Championship in 1860 that golf's popularity spread.

There was also an interest in football, and rules were introduced to regulate the number of players, the length of matches and the size of pitches. The Scottish Football Association was founded in 1873. Glasgow Rangers Football Club was formed in 1872, and its rival, Celtic, in 1888. For the first time, sport attracted large crowds of spectators who could travel around the country using the railways.

Toys like these were expensive, so many children had to invent games for playing in the streets and closes.

In 1883, the Scottish Amateur Athletic Association was formed to encourage athletics in private schools and universities.

Cycling became popular in the 1890s and many cycling clubs were formed. Cycling allowed people to escape from the city to the fresh air of the countryside. In 1839, a Scottish blacksmith, Kirkpatrick Macmillan, had invented the first pedal-powered bicycle.

Later Victorian 'safety cycles' were based on his design and had pneumatic tyres, invented by the Scotsman John Boyd Dunlop in 1888. Bicycles today still follow the basic Victorian designs.

Railway companies developed some of the first package holidays, taking city people to the coast where they could then board a paddle steamer. Glaswegians went 'doon the watter' to seaside resorts on the River Clyde, while the people in Edinburgh headed for the sandy beaches of Portobello. New resorts, such as Largs, Dunoon and Rothesay, were developed on the Clyde coast.

Victorian golfers teeing off at St Andrews.

Scots Abroad

Victorian Scots stand out for their contributions throughout the world. Many Scottish people at this time showed a great determination to be successful.

When faced with the upheavals of the Clearances, Highlanders realized that they had to adapt. Some went into the armed forces. Scottish regiments became a strong force in the British Army, earning a colourful and courageous reputation. They fought in many of the important wars and rebellions during this period, such as the Crimean War, and in conflicts in India and other parts of the British Empire.

Dr David Livingstone 1813–73

Born in Blantyre in Lanarkshire, Livingstone worked in a cotton mill from the age of ten. As well as attending school in the evening, after work, he tried to read books inside the mill, propping them up on the machinery. He went on to study medicine at Anderson College in Glasgow and then joined the London Missionary Society. He first went to Africa in 1840 and set up a mission in a country now called Botswana. Livingstone then began exploring the vast continent of Africa. In 1849, he crossed the Kalahari Desert, and over the next few years his exploration of the Zambesi River led to him seeing many wonderful sights. He named the most spectacular one, a great waterfall, after the queen – Victoria Falls. During his last exploration, in search of the sources of the Congo and Nile rivers, Livingstone died. His carefully recorded notes helped map out Africa in the nineteenth century and expand the British Empire.

The famous words, 'Doctor Livingstone, I presume', were spoken in 1871 by an American journalist, H. J. Stanley, upon finding Livingstone at Lake Tanganyika in Africa. People had not heard from Livingstone and thought he was dead.

Other Scottish families emigrated to begin a new life abroad. They went to America, Canada, Australia and New Zealand. Often they took little with them other than their Scottish identity, which they were keen to preserve. Andrew Carnegie, who became one the richest men in the world was the son of a Dunfermline linen weaver. They both emigrated to America in the 1840s. Carnegie created his massive fortune in the building of railways and in the manufacture of steel. Carnegie's generous donations helped establish public library systems in America, Canada and Britain.

Another famous Scot abroad was Alexander Graham Bell, the inventor of the telephone, who lived in the USA.

The Mosi-oa-Tunga falls in Zimbabwe. Livingstone renamed them Victoria Falls after Queen Victoria.

Andrew Carnegie is often described as a philanthropist. This means that he used his money to help those less well off than himself.

Victorian Style

There were many styles of dress through Victoria's reign. Fashions often changed, just as they do today. For most of Victoria's reign, women wore large, crinoline skirts that used whalebone cages to support them. A wealthy lady was able to buy carefully detailed dresses made in expensive fabrics such as silk, taffeta and velvet. The poor had to make do with coarsely woven cloth in simpler styles. In men's fashions, too, the differences were clear between rich and poor, mainly in the detailing and quality of fabric.

Victorian architecture was sometimes very elaborate, taking ideas from many different styles and countries. This was partly due to the influence of travel in the British Empire, with people taking ideas from buildings they had seen around the world and putting them together in different ways. Many wealthy people brought home designs to create buildings that included details of foreign architecture. There were many different combinations of styles. Victorian furniture also reflected this taste for elaborate decoration.

The Prince and Princess of Wales and their children have worn Scottish outfits for this photograph. The Royal Family made tartan fashionable for Victorians wear. Queen Victoria even designed her own tartan.

Charles Rennie Mackintosh 1868–1923

Charles Rennie Mackintosh was born in Glasgow. He worked in an architect's office and attended evening classes in the Glasgow School of Art. He won many prizes for his work. In 1895, the art school needed a new building and Mackintosh won a competition to design it. Working with his artist wife, Margaret MacDonald, they designed many house interiors.

Mackintosh rejected the elaborate decoration of Victorian architecture in favour of clean, simple lines. This became known as 'The Glasgow Style' and is easily recognizable through its soft tones of green, grey, pink and white, and simple decorations.

Mackintosh's influence was seen in the Glasgow International Exhibition of 1901, where his designs were being adapted for ordinary homes. People used factory-produced stained glass, furniture and wallpaper to recreate 'The Glasgow Style'.

Mackintosh designed the interiors for Kate Cranston's Tea-rooms, helping his work to become well-known in Glasgow. Tea-rooms became a fashionable part of city life as people met for lunch or afternoon tea. By using an exciting and different young architect to design her tea-rooms, Cranston was very successful. Sadly, many of Mackintosh's buildings have now been demolished.

Mackintosh's work was also exhibited in Europe and influenced many artists and architects in the twentieth century. He was often regarded as being ahead of his time as his designs were so different from the popular Victorian style. Mackintosh's work marks the end of the Victorian period and the beginning of a new era.

Mackintosh's simple, clean interiors contrasted greatly with traditional, heavily decorated Victorian styles.

Glossary

Close The place of entry from the street into a tenement building.

Coal-bearer Someone who carries coal to the top of the pit. This was usually a woman's job.

Colliery The area containing a coal-mine and the buildings that surround it.

Corsets Victorian underwear worn around the waist by women and girls.

Crimean War A war fought against Russia by Britain, France, Sardinia and Turkey (1853–56).

Crofting A Scottish word for farming a small piece of land.

Dockers People, usually men, who work on the harbour unloading and loading ships.

Estates Large areas of land owned by people called landlords. Each piece of land usually contains a large house.

Eviction Forcing people out of their homes and off their land by law.

Foundries Places where metal goods are made.

Hew Cut with a tool, such as an axe.

Highland Clearances The period from 1760 to 1866 when Highlanders were forced off their land by their landlords.

Hutches Carts used for carrying coal.

Ice boxes These looked like kitchen dressers. Each ice box had a block of ice on one side and food on the other.

Industrial Revolution A period of change during the 18th and 19th centuries when Britain became affected by industrialization.

Jute A rough material used in sacking and other heavy-duty products.

Mangle A machine that pressed out excess water from washed clothes by passing them between two heavy rollers.

Midden A rubbish or waste dump.

Parish An area that contains a church and the village or town around it.

Piecers People, usually children, who mend broken threads in a textile mill.

Pneumoconiosis A disease that caused great difficulty in breathing and stopped people from working.

Poorhouse A place where the very poor could live if they had nowhere else to go.

Textile mills Factories where cloth was made.

Trade unions Groups of workers joined together to try and improve working conditions and pay.

Tutors Teachers who were employed privately by a family to teach their children.

Ventilated When a room has a way of letting air into it.

Washboard A board with a rough metal surface on which wet laundry was scrubbed to get rid of dirt.

Wash-houses Buildings where people could wash their dirty laundry.

Wynd A Scottish word meaning a narrow alleyway.

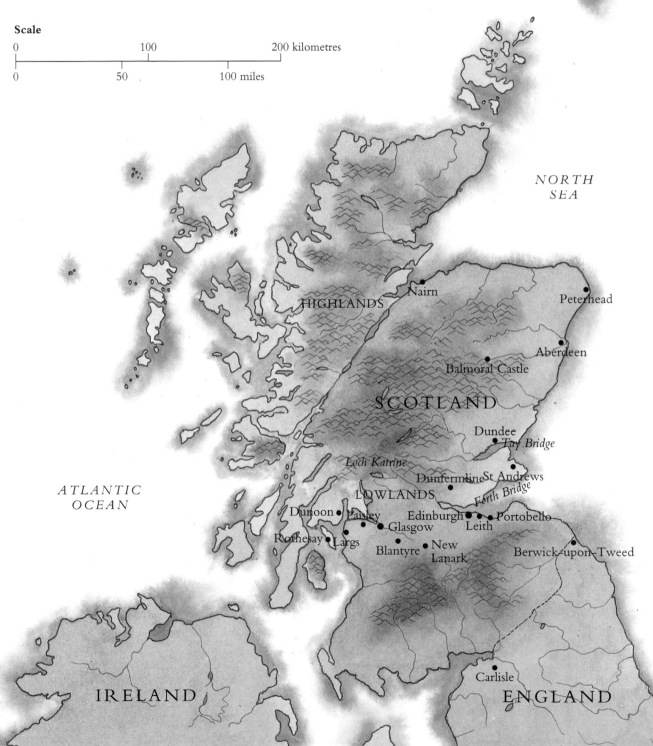

Map of Scotland

including places mentioned in the text

Scale

0   100   200 kilometres

0   50   100 miles

NORTH SEA

HIGHLANDS

Nairn

Peterhead

Aberdeen

Balmoral Castle

SCOTLAND

Dundee

Tay Bridge

Loch Katrine

Dunfermline   St Andrews

LOWLANDS

Forth Bridge

ATLANTIC OCEAN

Dunoon   Paisley   Edinburgh   Portobello

Glasgow   Leith

Rothesay   Largs

Blantyre   New Lanark   Berwick-upon-Tweed

Carlisle

IRELAND

ENGLAND

Further Information

Books to Read

Donald Gunn, *The Highland Clearances* (Wayland, 1993)

Iain Rose, *Children of Coal and Iron* (Wayland, 1996)

For photographs from the time:
Sydney Wood, *Scottish Life, 1750 to Recent Times* (Stanley Thornes, 1995)

Places to Visit

There are many museums and galleries throughout Scotland, providing a range of information on the Victorians. Your local museum will have Victorian photographs and artefacts from your area.

National Trust for Scotland has many properties, including:
Angus Folk Museum, Glamis, Forfar
The Hill House, Helensburgh
Robert Smail's Printing Works, Inverleithen
The Tenement House, Helensburgh
Weaver's Cottage, Kilbarchan
For further information contact the National Trust Scotland, 5 Charlotte Square, Edinburgh EH2 4DU. Tel: 0131 226 5922

David Livingstone Centre, 165 Station Road, Blantyre, Lanarkshire G72 9BT. Tel: 01698 823140.

Dundee Industrial Heritage Ltd, Verdant Works, West Henderson's Wynd, Dundee, DD2 5BT. Tel: 01382 225 282.

Grampian Transport Museum, Alford, Aberdeenshire AB3 8AD. Tel: 019755 62292.

Hunterian Museum and Art Gallery, University of Glasgow, University Avenue, Glasgow G12 8QQ. Tel: 0141 3305431.

Museum of Childhood, 42 High Street, Edinburgh, Lothian EH1 1TG. Tel: 0131 225 1131.

Museum of Education, Scotland Street, Glasgow G5 8QB. Tel: 0141 429 1202.

Museum of Transport, Kelvin Hall, 1 Bunhouse Road, Glasgow. Tel: 0141 287 2000.

Nairn Fishertown Museum, Laing Hall, Union Street, Nairn, Inverness-shire. Tel: 01667 456791.

New Lanark, World Heritage Centre, Lanark, Lanarkshire ML11 9DB. Tel: 01555 661345.

People's Palace Museum, Glasgow Green, Glasgow G40 1AT. Tel: 0141 554 0223.

Scottish Mining Museum, Lady Victoria Colliery, Newtongrange, Midlothian EH22 7QN. Tel: 0131 663 7519.

Summerlee Heritage Trust, West Canal Street, Coatbridge, Lanarkshire ML5 1QB. Tel: 01236 431261.

Index